Survivors:
Hungarian Jewish Poets
of the Holocaust

Survivors:
Hungarian Jewish Poets
of the Holocaust
Edited and translated
by Thomas Ország-Land

Smokestack Books
PO Box 408, Middlesbrough TS5 6WA
e-mail: info@smokestack-books.co.uk
www.smokestack-books.co.uk

Cover image: Budapest January 1945 (courtesy Krisztián Ungváry)
Author photo: Hajnalka Friebert

ISBN 978-0-9927409-2-4

Middlesbrough
moving forward

Smokestack Books is represented
by Inpress Ltd

for Isaac, Jude,
Ethan and Joseph

Contents

About Poetry and the Holocaust

This anthology of Holocaust poetry contains some of the best work of my teachers, friends and colleagues in my English translation, as well as my own written originally in English. All its authors either foresaw or survived the Holocaust, looked evil in the face and dedicated their lives to fighting racism in all its manifestations.

The book had its inception nearly half a century ago when at long last I had succeeded in writing English poetry to my satisfaction, and I set out to learn how to do it properly by translating the poetry of my betters from my native Hungarian into English. The poems may perhaps assist the descendents of the perpetrators, and of their victims and of the passive bystanders of the Holocaust to confront our dreadful joint inheritance together and build societies free of racial, religious and even gender intolerance for their own offspring.

Societies are very flexible. They adapt to meet the changing demands of the times. That is how humanity managed to conquer the Ice Age, virtually naked and unarmed against enormous odds, and recently even to survive the Cold War. The formerly slave-owning society of the United States today has a black president. Germany, the original home of Nazism, has built a healthy, decent, tolerant and wealthy society in the spirit of *Nie Wieder!* (Never again), despite the recent prolonged world recession encouraging an upsurge of racist extremism everywhere.

I was a child survivor of the Hungarian Holocaust as well as the three-month Soviet siege of Nazi-occupied Budapest, one of the longest and bloodiest city sieges that civilians have ever endured in Europe. My friendship with some of the contributors to this anthology originates from that time.

György Faludy was my teacher most of my life and my close friend towards the end of his.   I met the poet Eszter Forrai in a ruined playground in besieged Budapest where Jewish ghetto children sometimes passed the time when the uniformed Hungarian Nazis were not looking; we were also among the very few survivors of a Fascist raid on a Red Cross relief shelter that ended in mass murder on the shore of the Danube. Vera Szöllős and I were labourers employed by the same factory after the Holocaust. Magda Székely was my friend and editor. I first encountered András Mezei in a camp for children recovering from the trauma of the Holocaust; we faced one another across the ideological divide of the subsequent 1956 anti-Soviet revolution; eventually we collaborated in the post-Communist reconstruction on the editorial board of a literary/political journal.

Several of these authors are now dead. I recently attended a London meeting of Holocaust survivors, people acutely aware that the very occurrence of that crime is vociferously being denied by a resurgent wave of new Nazis who would like to repeat it. These last surviving witnesses know that they will be silenced soon by age and illness. They fear that, when they are gone, no one will be left to defend the world against such renewed barbarity.

I do not fear that. I believe that, as Odysseus will sail the seven seas of imagination in Homer's hexameters for the rest of history, so the passionate warnings of the Holocaust witnesses will resound through the ages in the surviving voices of the poets of our own time.

A close friend, a great English poet, has asked me how I have managed to find so many eloquent and powerful poems unknown to the rest of the world in one small, backward East European country like Hungary. I do not know the answer. But the real question is bigger: how could a small minority culture now comprising perhaps 1% of Hungary's 10 million population have produced such poets as these, as well as the creators of the computer (Neumann), the atom bomb (Szilárd), holography (Dénes), the British film industry (Korda) and even the ball-point pen (Bíró)?

There are in fact very few good Holocaust poems accessible to English readers, and for very sound reasons. The deed was done outside the English-speaking world. Its perpetrators succeeded in destroying many poems as well as their authors. The few survivors were concerned at the time mostly with survival, not poetry. Those who did write and survived to publish wrote mostly in languages other than English. And those who translate such works into English today tend to be academics rather than poets.

The post-Holocaust poets also tend to be silent on the subject simply because it is too big. How could you express appropriate disapproval, without sounding absurdly pretentious or obvious, at the premeditated murder of an entire people attempted in a manner quite well researched yet entirely beyond your own modest comprehension?

Survivors often weigh their task in different terms. They mourn their dead and regard their own broken lives with the pain true to the very moment of injury. The authors of this book lack a thirst for revenge. They record with gratitude the acts of generosity and courage to which they owe their lives. They recall the loss, the hunger, the fear, the humiliation to which they were once subjected, share their experience and make it accessible to the twenty-first century reading public.

But their poetry has been largely suppressed, ignored or misinterpreted by the servile literary establishment of Eastern Europe, the scene of the most appalling crimes, during the seven decades since the Holocaust. Both the Soviet-dominated governments of the region and their post-Communist successors have sought to minimize the enduring culpability of their countries by masquerading as the victims rather than the perpetrators of the crime. Their stance is undermined by the poems because they tell a different story.

Consider the work of great writers like Faludy as well as Jenő Heltai, Frigyes Karinthy and Ernő Szép, much loved and admired in their native Hungary (though hardly known abroad). They could not be ignored at home – but their Holocaust poetry has been consistently treated by school teachers, editors and critics as general anti-war protest in line with the perennial pious indignation of the post-war governments of the day. Even their readers do not know that these are Holocaust poets.

Even Miklós Radnóti, probably the greatest among the Holocaust poets and at last winning a rapidly growing, robust literary reputation in the West, was treated until very recently as one of 'the war poets' who fell victim to 'a tragic event' rather than to a deliberate act of racist murder committed by the regular Hungarian Army at the approval or at least connivance of the country's vocal anti-Semitic majority. The Holocaust literature of some other writers in this anthology, such as Éva Láng and Mezei and Szöllős, can be ignored in Hungary more easily because their authors began to release it only recently, late in life.

Worse is to come. Pandering to the aggressive current rise of anti-Semitism, an ultra-Conservative, populist Hungarian government recently enacted a new constitution repudiating any legal as well as moral responsibility for the Holocaust murder of some half a million of the country's citizens – mostly Jews and also Roma, homosexuals and political dissidents – committed by the Hungarian state in collaboration with Nazi Germany.

The new law does not deny the Holocaust. It attempts to shift the blame on Germany for all the Holocaust crimes committed in Hungary since the year 1944 when a token German military force was welcomed in the country by a still independent Hungarian government. All judges as well as teachers and museum curators employed by state institutions face dismissal if they depart from the official line.

The government has also included several anti-Semitic authors in the national school curriculum. It has tacitly encouraged demands by far-Right organizations for the official rehabilitation of Second World War leader Miklós Horthy. In the worst tradition of East European authoritarianism, it has just set up a state historical research institution intended to rewrite history.

Outrageous claims already made by the new so-called Veritas institute fly in the face of credible research into the painstaking marginalization, dispossession, ghettoization and eventual deportation of significant population groups to slave-labour and death camps carried out by the Hungarian authorities. Its assertions trivializing the country's role in the Holocaust are contradicted by numerous eyewitness accounts of cheerful civilians descending on the abandoned Jewish homes in many communities to rob them even before their owners were crammed into the deportation trains by the authorities for Auschwitz.

Professor Randolph L. Braham of City University, New York, the doyen of Holocaust studies, and the Nobel Laureate Elie Wiesel have both returned high state honours awarded to them by the Hungarian government in protest over its attempts to falsify history. Both are Holocaust survivors and hugely influential American writers of Hungarian origin well disposed towards Hungary.

Some of the world's leading scholars have called on Hungary to refrain from using their names in connection with its current official Holocaust Memorial Year. Several Jewish-Hungarian organizations have decided to boycott official memorial ceremonies planned to mark this year's 70th anniversary of the German 'invasion'.

This could be the first occasion that the deeply divided, weakened and humbled Jewish community comprising mostly Holocaust survivors and their descendents at last dares to deploy its collective will to oppose the authorities. This could also deliver a death blow to the ailing image of post-Communist Hungary, a nascent member of the European Union, as a functioning European democracy.

Professor István Deák, a widely respected Hungarian historian at Columbia University, New York, observes: 'I cannot overstate how much Hungary would gain in its international standing if, after all the deceitful evasions since the war, it would at last face up to its responsibilities from the past.' Such a development would also benefit Hungary immeasurably by freeing society of the burden of suppressed guilt that still weighs down its conscience over the shameful record of its recent past.

Jewish-Hungarian community leaders frequently remind their Western visitors that, contrary to the conventional reckoning of historians, the Holocaust did not begin with the gas chambers. The road to Auschwitz was long and clearly signposted for all who cared to look.

Feeding from the deep regional roots of racial and religious intolerance, Europe's first modern anti-Semitic law was passed in Hungary in 1920, severely restricting the number of Jews admitted to higher education. Faludy was among those affected. The *Numerus clausus* (Restricted numbers) legislation led to frequent, bloody atrocities at the universities and an exodus of brilliant Jewish students to earn their qualifications in the West, eventually winning a string of Nobel prizes for Hungary. Many of them, including such other giants as the novelist Arthur Koestler and the nuclear physicist Ede Teller, never returned to their homeland.

Radnóti responded to Hitler's rise to power in 1933 by writing *The Bull*, declaring that 'I will struggle and... fall when the hour is come,/and the district will treasure my bones for reminders to future ages.' And by the time Tamás Emőd wrote his desperate *Deluge* in 1938, the German medical profession had already performed 400,000 sterilization operations on victims chosen for their supposed physical as well as racial inferiority. The doctors had also participated in the extra-judicial murder of 1% of the entire German population in the national euthanasia programme, directly preparing the ground for the annihilation of Jews by industrial means.

Many Holocaust survivors, including the poets Primo Levi and Paul Celan, committed suicide after the war, perhaps because they saw no room left for decency, let alone a future, after Auschwitz. Some have turned to poetry to shout out their grief and rage at their incomprehensible humiliation and abuse at the hands of the Nazis, for which they had been totally unprepared.

The subsequent generations are not unprepared. They are all survivors, and their enduring capacity for love and decency originates from within. But they now must learn to live with the astounding technological capacities available to all societies to attempt genocide – and the leaders of some are openly fantasizing about that. We are even deploying our technology to destroy nature, of which we are part.

My own experience tells me that humanity's one chance today lies in total dedication to survival, untrammelled by the guilt, the grief, the resentments of the past. We must literally talk and cry them out of our system.

Poetry is a great vehicle of post-crisis reconciliation. The work of these Holocaust masters may teach the future how to heal the wounds of the past.

Thomas Ország-Land, Budapest, 2014

Thomas Ország-Land

Caution

in memoriam Jaroslav Ježek

Our civilizations
have sown new notions
of treating unwanted
populations...
thus reasoned
a seasoned
child of a death camp,
thus entreating
you – and the future:

You' ll lose all you own.
Even life is on loan.
Don't cry. Be cautious.
Be canny. Be clever,
and never, but never,
but never forget it.
And, boldly
hold up your head
...while you've got it.

Jenő Heltai

Ars Poetica

Do not wait till you're invited.
Poet, claim your place
on the rostrum. Warn the neighbours
of the threat they face.

Share your heart with their cold world.
Share each fear, each scar.
Shed your armour, shed your clothes:
show all that you are.

Do not wait until you're silenced
never to sing again.
Never, ever, hold your tongue.
Bellow out your pain.

Watch the racist rabble-rousers.
Mark the lies they spawn –
The night is long and dark and deadly,
but expect the dawn.

Slanders hurt... but your song is true.
It will outlive any lie.
Drink up your poison if you must,
but sing until you die.

Magda Székely

Saving the Sodomites

I hold a solitary vigil
over this forsaken garden
of bones. The skulls have called my name.
It is my lot to guard them.

The Lord once called a prophet's name.
He answered, and the ossified,
dead flesh began to grow again.
Behold, the hecatombs revived.

I do not possess the power
to grow live flesh upon dead bone.
This time, though, I call the questions.
No-one answers. I'm alone.

What's the use of retribution
over swiftly passing time?
Can you exercise forgiveness
if all deny the crime?

The fragile stalk of trust can feed
from just thin air. I'll never tire
to seek 10 righteous Sodomites
...to save this city from the fire.

András Mezei

Roads

I

You're lost in grief abroad
forever –
in cobblestones, asphalt.
The hostile god of the land
swoops down upon you.

You know your life is only
the road to resurrection:
certainly.
And your belief
brings no relief.

II

The columns shrunk – for the frail ones fell behind
or sought survival by scooping up some snow
to quench their thirst in the mountains along the route
to Dachau, or briefly stooped to tighten their boots
or pick up a snail or a fistful of grass or rape
to fill their mouths and fool their famished stomachs.

Such people often died in the constant fire
provoked by their looting and insubordination...
like mother, caught with clover filling her mouth,
and sister, with crushed snails in her gaping mouth.
Their corpses were left among the fruit of the fields,
among the snails, the grass, the rape, the clover.

Some 13,000 civilian captives dispatched
on a 300km march
that took 8 days. Some 1,800 arrived.

Miklós Radnóti

Deathmarch

Collapsed exhausted, only a fool would rise again
to drag his knees and ankles once more like marching pain
yet press on as though wings were to lift him on his way,
invited by the ditch but in vain, he'd dare not stay...
Ask him, why not? Maintaining his pace, he might reply:
he longs to meet the wife and a gentler death. That's why.
But he's insane, that poor man, because above the homes,
since we have left them, only a scorching whirlwind roams.
The walls are laid. The plum tree is broken. And the night
lurks bristling as a frightened, abandoned mongrel might.
Oh, if I could believe that all things for which I yearn
exist beyond my heart, that there's still home and return...
return! the old veranda, the peaceful hum of bees
attracted by the cooling fresh plum jam in the breeze,
the still, late summer sunshine, the garden drowsing mute,
among the leaves the swaying voluptuous naked fruit,
and Fanni waiting for me, blonde by the russet hedge,
while languidly the morning re-draws the shadow's edge...
It may come true again – see, the moon, so round! – be wise...
Don't leave me, friend, shout at me, shout! and I will arise!

Thomas Ország-Land

Epilogue

Unmarked the moment when our forebears lost
our innocence to automated killing.
The prisoners' feet were kissed by winter frost.
Their hunger ached. Some gave up hope, unwilling
to stumble on with pride and will run out.

They deemed a small delay a meagre prize,
fell gently and remained there calm and solemn,
unless one were to shout at them to rise,
awaiting death behind the marching column –
Some people had the stubborn strength to shout.

They've left to us the throb of phantoms' feet
and principles esteemed by every nation,
a world of wealthy customers to eat
the feast of plenty set by automation –
and now and then a fearful, halting doubt:

when warplanes scrape across the sky a scar
above our loved ones' heads or when the telly
brings for our entertainment from afar
a child with hunger bloated in the belly –
and we have lost the voice or will to shout.

György Faludy

The Germans' Mercenaries

Hey-ho!... we are that shabby lot,
the Germans' infamous mercenaries,
who do not care if the officers march us
over the mountains or down the plain
to slaughter peasants or lords or priests
for fun or gain or the hangman's rope.
We have campaigned on all terrains,
laid waste to land and lives and churches,
and torched the city of Breda and chased
its terrified children fleeing the flames
because we are that shabby lot,
the Germans' infamous mercenaries.

Have you seen an innocent child
raided by marauding soldiers?
That is how we were pressed into service
and fitted out with flags and armour
and trained by the whip that made us fit
for our shameful trade, hey-ho! –
tormenting you when you're defenceless,
smashing your infant's head on your wall,
invading your bed, abusing you in it,
avoiding a fight when we cannot win it,
because we are that shabby lot,
the Germans' infamous mercenaries.

We've devastated seven counties
and climbed the seven hills of Rome
and taken a blood bath in the heat
and taken a mud bath in the autumn
and waded across vast snowbound fields
and quenched our thirst by filthy snow,
and we baked to the south of the River Po
and swam like rats across the Meuse
and fed on locusts and fallen horses
and heard and uttered horrible curses
because we are that shabby lot,
the Germans' infamous mercenaries.

We recognize no father, mother,
we cut down every apple tree
and poison every well we find
and serve any master who pays us well.
Without a word, or thought or even
hatred, we guzzle up your wine
and seize and cart away your chattels,
and kidnap, rape and sell your child...
and you must thank us before we go
or we shall brain you by your gate
because we are that shabby lot,
the Germans' infamous mercenaries.

The years march on like mercenaries...
Dismissed from service mercilessly,
one day we'll doze, old fools, on benches,
too frail to bear old Frundsberg's blade.
We'll drag our ailing hulks in pain
on weary feet beset by gout,
from fort to court and meekly seek
your charity: just a crust of bread
and just a scrap of love to last us
until the final port where the devil
wonders: *Where is that useless lot,
the Germans' infamous mercenaries?*

Hey-ho!... we are that shabby lot,
the Germans' infamous mercenaries,
who do not care *(...Reprise)*

Tamás Emőd

Message in a Bottle

Beneath a rig of groans, in a tempest of tears,
engulfed by fear as an awesome deluge recurs,

on board a lost and battered, rudderless galley
afloat on the blood of this dreadful time of folly –

like sailors who trust their news to a bottle in the current,
I thrust these final verses into the torrent

so that, beyond death and terror and darkness, you
may still receive them one day in a better future,

you, in whom we have placed our faith and hopes
in vain, for we shall never reach your shores:

free shores, our home ever since the centaurs' idylls,
cultured Europe, our ancient, classical cradle.

* * *

We signal our final farewells before the night covers us,
our helpless pleas of distress flashed over the flood,

and still salute the offspring of tomorrow,
we the galley slaves of the present, the ship and the oars

whose festive garlands have been torn away,
we sad and sensitive souls of this brutal age

who have foretold the worst and seen it all
who had screamed out in fear before we fell,

the children lusting for wisdom, humour and trust
before the depth of hell roared over us:

before our plight sinks into blind oblivion,
I send you these lines, the final news of our lives.

* * *

Beyond the final Capes of Good Hope of existence,
chained to the galley's oar-bench beneath the mast,

we still survive like beasts in filthy stables,
abused as apes are, locked up in a cage,

our ears are cocked, our fur is bristling with fear
but silence! the guards assault us through the bars,

our human pride destroyed, we huddle dismayed,
we have consumed... even our flesh and blood,

we know that all our endeavours must be in vain,
that we must perish without release or escape:

despite the lights we've lit here forever, you
have abandoned your children, cultured Europe!

* * *

Beneath a rig of groans, in a tempest of tears,
engulfed by fear as an awesome deluge recurs,

like sailors who trust their news to a bottle in the current,
I thrust these final verses into the torrent

that bears me towards the jaws of fate through the spray
...here, in the year of 1938.

Ernő Szép

The Truth

The truth is that they lie to you
inciting docile folks to hatred.
Resist, resist, resist their truth
of infamy, of ruthlessness.

The newspapers project a lie.
They twist the truth and peddle drivel
and spew their raving explanations
to kindle mass hysteria.

They're teasing you. It's all a game.
It's not just on your mind. Resist it.
You must have lost your sense and faith
if you can chew it and digest it.

Resist, resist such wickedness.
Insist: Their truth is odious!
And have the strength to ridicule
the preachers of such lunacy.

Close up, retreat, escape from here,
protect yourself from their corruption,
from their polluted mist of truths that
consumes unguarded souls alive.

Resist, you hear!... what's foul and ugly,
and what torments and nauseates you.
To see the truth, behold the spring and
your features in your photograph...

For truth appears in mirth and youth,
in consolation and assistance,
in tenderness and in affection,
in pard'n-me, in thank-you-kindly.

For truth is found down in this world
in friendship only and attention
and in persistent, robust love
whose very roots spring from the heart.

For truth is beauty, truth is goodness.
For truth dwells in your own sweet dreams.
It is absent from fickle fashion.
The truth is, truth will last forever.

They've struck their knives in you... but even
should they tear out our entrails,
while we can breathe, while we can think,
we must resist, resist their deed.

I seize you by the wrists, my friend.
Look in my eyes! I scream: Resist it!
Insist upon your innocence!
Defend your truth! Do not surrender!

Be strong, be straight, be wise, a hero,
or shield your truth in drink or madness,
or view this frenzy from without
like God... if God does not exist.

Miklós Radnóti

The Bull

Hitherto, I lived the throbbing life of a youthful bull
bored in the noonday heat among pregnant cows in the field,
running around in unending circles declaring his powers
and waving amid his game a foaming flag of saliva.
He shakes his head and turns with the splitting, thick air on his horns
and behind his stamping hooves the tormented grass and earth
spatters widely about the terrified green pasture.

And still I live like a bull, but a bull that suddenly stops
in the heart of the meadow singing with crickets, stops nostrils lifted
and sniffing the air. For he senses that far in the mountain forests
the roebuck too stops and listens and lightly flees with the wind,
the hissing wind that carries the stench of a distant wolf pack –
thus the bull snorts, but he will not escape like the deer
and considers that when his time is to come, he will fight and fall
and his bones will be scattered about in the district by the horde –
and slowly and sadly the bull bellows through the fat air.

Thus I will struggle and thus I will fall when the hour is come,
and the district will treasure my bones for reminders to future ages.

Miklós Radnóti

War Diary, 1935–36

I: Monday Evening

These days the distant news dissolves the world
and often brings your heart to miss a beat – but
the trees of old still hold your childhood secrets
in their widening memory rings.

Between suspicious mornings and furious nights,
you have spent half your life corralled by war.
Upon the glinting points of the bayonets, striding
repression encircles you.

The land of your poetry may appear in your dreams
with the wings of freedom gliding above the meadows,
still sensed through the mist, and when the magic breaks
the elation may persist.

But you half-sit on your chair when you rarely dare
to work... restrained in grey and fearful mire.
Your hand still dignified by the pen moves forward,
more burdened day by day.

View the tide of clouds: the ravenous thunderhead
of the war is devouring the gentle blue of the sky.
With her loving, protective arms around you
sobs your anxious bride.

II: Tuesday Evening

I can sleep calmly now, and methodically
I go about my business... despite the gas,
grenades and bombs and aircraft made to kill me.
I'm past the fear, the rage. I cannot cry.
So I have come to live as hard as teams
of road-builders high among the windy hills:
when their light shelters
decay with age,
they build new shelters
and soundly sleep in beds of fragrant wood-shavings
and splash and dip their faces at dawn in cool
and radiant streams.

* * *

I spy out from this hilltop where I live:
the clouds are crowding.
As the watch on the mainmast over stormy seas
will bellow when, by a lightning's flash, at last
he thinks he sees
a distant land,
I also can discern from here the shores of peace:
I shout: *Compassion!*
...My voice is light.

The chilly stars respond with a brightening light,
my word is carried far by the chilly breeze
of the deepening night.

III: Weary Afternoon

A slowly dying wasp flies through the window.
My woman dreaming... muttering in her sleep.
The clouds are turning brown. Along their edges
caressed by the breeze, white ripples teem.

What can I say?... The winter comes and war comes.
I shall fall broken, abandoned without any reason
and worm-ridden earth will fill my mouth and eye-pits
and through my corpse, fresh roots will sprout.

* * *

Oh, peaceful, swaying afternoon, lend me your calm!
I too must rest for a while, I will work later.
Your sunrays hang suspended from the shrubs
as the evening saunters across the hill.

The blood of a fine fat cloud has smeared the sky.
And beneath the burning leaves, the scented yellow
berries are ripening, swelling with wine.

IV: Evening Approaches

The sun is descending down a slippery sky.
The evening is approaching early, sprawling
along the road. The watchful moon has missed it.
Pools of mist are falling.

The evening's whirling sounds among the branches
grow louder. The hedges wake to turn and tilt
at weary travellers. These lines clasp one another
as they are slowly built.

And now!.. a squirrel invades my quiet room
and runs two brown iambic lines, a race
of terror between my window and the wall
and flees without a trace.

My fleeting peace has vanished with the squirrel.
Outside in the fields, the vermin silently spread,
digesting slowly the endless, regimented,
reclining rows of the dead.

Tamás Emőd

Only You

Despite your barefaced lying
despite your naked lewdness
and in your degradation
and in your destitution,
with obdurate defiance
I fear for you, I love you,
you easy slut, my poppet,
my only, only life.

Tamás Emőd

Distinction

Generous age, how you burn to trace
the race of your humble, itinerant son!
Allow me to make a gift in return.
Take this book, before I pass on.

Miklós Radnóti

The Witness

I am a poet, and I would be rejected
even if I fell silent in disgrace,
∪ - ∪ - ∪ - but lots of devils
are happy to sing in my place.

I have provoked, believe me, every caution,
suspicion sniffing after me like a sleuth!
I am a poet destined for the stake,
a witness who tells the truth.

A poet – one who notes what he has seen,
that snow is white and blood and poppies red
and that the poppies' downy stems are green.

One whose own blood shall at last be spilled
...for I have never killed.

György Faludy

Refugee, 1940

Like our hosts, we thought the French army
was the mightiest under the sun.
And what did it show to the German Nazis?
Beaten backsides on the run.

The French distrust and despise us aliens
for fleeing to their land for salvation.
It was their own deceit, not ours,
that callously brought down this nation.

They boast: defeat will bring them peace
(too bad for the Jews). Oh, hunky-dory...
Few of them know that it's only the start
and very far from the end of the story.

The Nazis will settle into their homes.
They'll drink their cellars dry, abuse
their women and, should they object,
treat their hosts as they treat the Jews.

Miklós Radnóti

The Third Eclogue

Pastoral muse! Accompany me to this sleepy coffeehouse
from the light-drenched riverbank and its burrowing, sightless
moles and their rising molehills... from the sunburnt fishermen
with white teeth and noble proportions, stretching out
asleep in their slippery barges after the morning catch!

My pastoral muse, accompany me to this urban district –
Those seven carousing travelling salesmen should not deter you:
pathetic lads, they are burdened by the pressures of business...
nor should those doctors of law to the right: not one of whom can
remember how to play the flute... how they suck their cigars!

Accompany me! I'm a teacher and, between classes, I've chosen
this place for a moment's peace in the smoke to ponder on passion.
A tweet from a tiny bird can rejuvenate an old poplar.
A call from a woman has lifted me high to the peaks of youth
and flung me back to the wild adolescent lands of desire.

My pastoral muse, assist me! Today, the triumphant trumpets
of dawn resounded in praise of the fleeting flash of her smile,
describing the feel and form and the heat and cool of her body,
and how it reflects the moon, and the way she gives herself,
and the joyful, dancing rhythm of sighs that escape her lips.

My pastoral muse, assist me! Allow me to serenade love
despite my nagging sadness, despite the unending pain
that hounds me through this world. I know I soon shall perish.
The trees grow awry and mine pits collapse and, in my dreams,
I hear that even the very bricks in the houses are screaming.

My pastoral muse, assist me! The poets are dying in droves.
The sky is collapsing on us. No mounds will guard our remains,
nor graceful urns like in classical times – only the odd
surviving poetic fragments. How then can I sing about love?
But... her body is beckoning. Pastoral muse, assist me!

István Vas

The Colours that Day

The soldier is tanned and blond, his car and tunic green.
His silken hound is brown and bright and cheerful.
Bound from Paris to Moscow, stranded here,
he regards our streets with mild but blatant loathing.

The traffic light turns red. The vehicle must stop.
The driver sighs, looks blank. His thoughts race far away.
A gent approaches, pandering to the German,
his balding bloated head aglow with zeal.

He speaks too loud: *Sie fahren nach Astoria?...*
He asks with feeling. But he is ignored.
He is bent to the window, his brow haloed in sweat,
proud to serve our grand and glorious ally.

The light has turned again to amber and to green.
The gent attending to the German fails to notice.
He waves his arms about, eliciting
impatient, disapproving reservation.

From the parting car, the hound still holds
our friendly guide in keen, Teutonic gaze.
The sun breaks through. Its yellow rays ignite
the identifying Yellow Stars Jews must display.

For a moment, the murder, the pain, the fear that smear
this, our 20th century after Jesus... and
even its savage heartbeat are suspended.
A newsboy cries out: *Normandy, Hey!* They've landed.

Vera Szöllős

Absence

...Then he gently closed the door. His absence
reverberates throughout the gaping home.
The coat my father did not take with him
still bears the skinny presence of his shape.

His instruments prepare themselves for action.
His books await his hand to turn the pages.
His barely opened packet of tobacco
reinvents his fiddling bony fingers.

The mottled mat extends towards his steps.
The mirror glints towards his specs. The lens
of his empty camera dimly stares.
The fragrance of his pipe still fills the drawer.

The hand of his voltmeter lying limp,
the power is disconnected... But his friend
has repaired the dodgy wireless,
and it has played the Scottish Symphony!

He's everywhere, and yet so far away.
Just sometimes, when I try to learn to live
with his absence, I still sense his breath
behind me as he softly strokes my hair.

Eszter Forrai

Christmas

Mistletoe glowing white like marbles,
bunched with tiny leaves.
Streets festooned with mistletoe.
The sight of graceful pinetrees.
I leave a grieving daughter's bouquet
upon an unknown grave.
And I remember the bars before me,
behind me, imagined and real.
Mother had filled the children's stomachs
with stolen cabbage leaves.
Sand grated under our teeth... We had
not even crusts of bread.
Beyond the bars, the guard is slowly
pacing along his path.
The pacing soldier's tunic is grey,
its buttons are glowing gold,
and we are waiting behind the bars.
I count the buttons. Eight.
His steps still echo through the yard.
Tonight they killed my father.

Éva Láng

Hungry

The pillow asleep on a troubled bunk.
Its dreams? Some well-seasoned, fragrant morsels.
The sweetness of puddings and rolls and cakes
        makes the soul yearn. For its wage.

Swallow? Swallow what? Only saliva
moistens the tongue, not mutton stew
and bean soup, braised kidneys and greens.
        Asleep is the palate. The teeth.

Is that a juicy joint on the boil?
And asparagus soup with golden pasta,
the glow of roast turkey? Does your mouth savour
        the flavour, the feel of potatoes?

Herbal honey tea, mint in the air lifts
lightly like lace. Tea brewed with my tears.
It's bitter. Sugar has never been in
        this grim, this rickety tin mug...

Cholent. The smoky taste of stuffed goose-necks
held by the beans, and the best of the legs.
The larder shelves laden, the storage bar sags.
        The poultry preserved in fat.

The pillow asleep, caressed by the dream.
The pot will never release it. Will
the communal kitchen spare me a scrap?
        I will stay here, even if starved!

Hanna Szenes

Spark

I

This spark would gladly burn out
by igniting a flame,

her life would be fulfilled
in a flame igniting a blaze.

This spark would gladly give all
for a blaze to light up the hearts,

a blaze to light up the world
and raise a hope for life.

II

Some seven steps, the length of this cell.
Two steps across. I can even tell
how long my life
will last.

A day or two, at the least. Or a week.
It might perhaps last out the month,
but I must not doubt
the end.

I won't be 23 in July.
I knew the risks. The stakes were high.
I played for life.
I lost.

György Timár

Games in the Cellar

from *The Calendar of Horror*, January 5, 1944

The spirit fights back by playing even as bullets threaten.
Love as well as mildew bloom in the air raid shelter.

Two awkward gestures. A fleeting kiss: dry but defiant.
Love, those about to die salute thee in their desire.

In the evening, the killers smash in the outer gate.
But we have Mr. Knöpfler, a former bubbly salesman.

He's bouncing forward, beaming: *Boys, how much for a postponement?*
For just 10 days of delay? I say, 10,000 in gold...

Just 10 days till liberation... We're calculating if
life will pass today this exam in salesmanship.

That' ll do! Shut your face! Pay up sharply: 10 days, 10,000. Of course.
Don't worry – we will yet turn you into a pretty corpse...

The textile dealer grumbles: *Why do I have to toss in,*
after the golden chains, my last, expensive sovereigns?

Let's play while we can. Let each one play an appropriate game.
I swear on eternal love. Mr. Knöpfler negotiates.

The cannon thunder. Smoke blacks out the firmament.
Knöpfler is smart. He reserves 5,000 until the end.

...But they marched him to the river and executed him later,
abandoning his corpse by the quayside, on the 10th day.

Thomas Ország-Land

Ghetto Games

I: The Promise

A grieving 5-year old
promised her rabbit:

*Don't cry,
little one!
When the soldiers
come to grab you...
I won't leave you.*

II: Well of Twilight

Beneath a gloomy square of the sky
  in the shadow of awesome, looming walls,
a crowd of kids met day after day
  to test, to learn in that well of twilight
which ones in the block were destined to die.

Just a few at a time. Our faces were grey
  and small, our eyes were clouded with fear.
We hung the Book and a key on a thread –
  for we understood the path of death
yet could not make it go away.

We huddled close with lonely dread
  in our hearts. The Bible turned around
and with it, the key. They came to rest
  at random to point at a ghetto child.
He would be the first among the dead.

The block has grown, the world progressed.
  I, the survivor, stand in the sunlight
aware of the cloud in every eye
  as fear of the future grips the globe,
rekindling doom in every breast.

Eszter Forrai

Steps

I: Orphaned Shores

Climbing or descending,
these steps of the river embankment,
these steep stone slabs of the quay
form a stairway up from the playful waves
towards the sun in the heavens
and the soothing quilt of the sky
that hold the world in warmth.

But then it was January
and the steps were cruelly cold,
the steps that led down to the icy Danube –
we were told to remove our shoes
and stand in barefooted lines
as the soldiers loaded their rifles
beneath the weeping sky.

The soldiers were not aiming toy guns.
The siege was not played out with toy bombs,
and we had not even time
to blow our dreams away –
And the infamy was witnessed
by the orphaned lines of the children's
shoes, awaiting our fate on the quay.

II: Sarah Walks

My daughter's very first steps...
A conquest, a leap to the target,
a ribbon-ripping, brilliant
epic triumph! My stumbling,
intrepid, robust princess
has boldly set out! Sarah walks.
Lo! Her frozen terrain
has come alive. The walls
around her have steadied. And,
to the sound of her hesitant steps,
I learn to adjust my life.

III: Sarah Dancing

Green is this rustic, lakeside world
that I've adopted,
with a riot of scattering silver pearls
of my daughter's laughter, the lines
of unfolding yellow water-lilies
and a glowing grey and green-blue sky.
I've brought ladybirds to ride them
over the deep –
The sky is turning somersaults,
its chuckles exploding in cheerful vapours;
but the evening trees below
are sighing, sighing gusts of storms.
Native to these woodland slopes,
we race across them.
Our healthy bodies pulse to our rhythm
and love of dancing, they whirl in step
with the music of bluebells.

IV: Birthday!

A volcano aged 16: the silent
flow of Sarah's yearning has burst.
My green-eyed daughter clasps to her breasts
a blue-eyed lad, and I watch from afar
the raging lava, the vapours, the flames,
the incandescent burning rocks
of her passion blasting skywards –
my daughter has turned 16 and embarked
on the Milky Way of adult emotions.

I behold the pulsating glow of her star,
I hearken to the pace of her heartbeat
from a distant planet by the waters
lapping against the steps of the quay.

Miklós Radnóti

Letter to my Wife

Mute worlds lie in the depths, their stillness crying
inside my head; I shout: no-one's replying
in war-dazed, silenced Serbia the distant,
and you are far away. My dreams, persistent,
are woven nightly in your voice, and during
the day it's in my heart still reassuring –
and thus I keep my silence while, profoundly
detached, the cooling bracken stirs around me.

No longer can I guess when I will see you,
who were once firm and sure as psalms can be – you,
as lovely as the shadow and the light – you,
whom I could seek out mute, deprived of sight – you,
now with this landscape you don't know entwined – you,
projected to the eyes, but from the mind – you,
once real till to the realm of dreams you fell – you,
observed from my own puberty's deep well – you,

nagged jealously in my soul for a truthful
pledge that you love me, that upon the youthful
proud peak of life you'll be my bride; I'm yearning
and then, with sober consciousness returning,
I do remember that you are my wife and
my friend – past three wild frontiers, terrified land.
Will autumn leave me here forgotten, aching?
My memory's sharper over our lovemaking;

I once believed in miracles, forgetting
their age; above me, bomber squadrons setting
against the sky where I just watched the spark and
the colour of your eyes – the blue then darkened,
the bombs then longed to fall. I live despite them
and I am captive. I have weighed up, item
by painful item, all my hopes still tended –
and will yet find you. For you, I've descended,

along the highways, down the soul's appalling
deep chasms. I shall transmit myself through falling
live flames or crimson coals to conquer the distance,
if need be learn the treebark's tough resistance –
the calm and might of fighting men whose power
in danger springs from cool appraisal shower
upon me, bringing sober strength anew,
and I become as calm as 2×2.

Miklós Radnóti

À la Recherche...

Gentle past evenings, you too are ennobled through recollection!
Brilliant table adorned by poets and their young women,
where have you slid in the mud of the memory? Where is the night
when the exuberant friends still merrily drank the native
wine of the land from slender glasses that sparkled their glances?

Lines of poetry swam around the glow of the lamps
and bright green adjectives swayed on the foaming crest of the metre
and still the dead were alive, the prisoners home, and the dear
vanished friends wrote verse, those fallen long ago whose hearts
lie under the soil of Spain and Flanders and Ukraine.

Some of them charged forward gritting their teeth in the fire and fought
only because there was nothing they could do to avoid it,
and while their company fitfully slept around them under
the soiled shelter of night, they remembered their rooms of the past,
calm caves and islands, their retreat from this society.

Some of them travelled helpless in sealed cattle trucks to places,
some stood numbly waiting unarmed in freezing minefields,
some also went voluntarily, silent with guns in their hands
for clearly they saw their personal place and role in the fighting –
now the angel of freedom guards their great dreams in the night.

Some... doesn't matter. Where have the wise, winy evenings vanished?
Swift swarmed the draftnotes and swift multiplied the poetic fragments
as did the wrinkles around the lips and eyes of the wives
with enchanting smiles. The elf-footed girls grew dull
and heavy in loneliness over the silent and endless war years.

Where is the night, the tavern and, under the lime trees, that table?
Where are the living and where are the others trampled in battle?
Still, my heart hears their voices, my hand still holds their handshakes,
thus I quote their works and behold their proportions and stature,
silent prisoner myself in Serbia's wailing mountains.

Where is the night? Such a night perhaps may never recur, for death
gives always a different perspective to all that has vanished.
They still sit at the table, they hide in the smiles of the women,
and they will sip from our glasses, the friends still unburied and waiting,
lying in distant forests, asleep in foreign pastures.

Miklós Radnóti

The Seventh Eclogue

Evening approaches the barracks, and the ferocious oak fence
braided with barbed wire, look, dissolves in the twilight.
Slowly the eye thus abandons the bounds of our captivity
and only the mind, the mind is aware of the wire's tension.
Even fantasy finds no other path towards freedom.
Look, my beloved, dream, that lovely liberator,
releases our aching bodies. The captives set out for home.

Clad in rags and snoring, with shaven heads, the prisoners
fly from Serbia's blinded peaks to their fugitive homelands.
Fugitive homeland! Oh – is there still such a place?
Still unharmed by bombs? As on the day we enlisted?
And will the groaning men to my right and my left return safely?
And is there a home where hexameters are appreciated?

Dimly groping line after line without punctuation,
here I write this poem as I live in the twilight, inching
like a bleary-eyed caterpillar, my way on the paper –
everything, torches and books, all has been seized by the *Lager*
guard, our mail has stopped and the barracks are muffled by fog.

Riddled with insects and rumours, Frenchmen, Poles, loud Italians,
separatist Serbs and dreamy Jews live here in the mountains –
fevered, a dismembered body, we lead a single existence,
waiting for news, a sweet word from a woman, and decency, freedom,
guessing the end still obscured by the darkness, dreaming of miracles.

Lying on boards, I am a captive beast among vermin,
the fleas renew their siege but the flies have at last retired.
Evening has come; my captivity, behold, is curtailed
by a day and so is my life. The camp is asleep. The moonshine
lights up the land and highlights the taut barbed wire fence,
it draws the shadow of armed prison guards, seen through the window,
walking, projected on walls, as they spy the night's early noises.

Swish go the dreams, behold my beloved, the camp is asleep,
the odd man who wakes with a snort turns about in his little space
and resumes his sleep at once, with a glowing face. Alone
I sit up awake with the lingering taste of a cigarette butt
in my mouth instead of your kiss, and I get no merciful sleep,
for neither can I live nor die without you, my love, any longer.

Miklós Radnóti

Picture Postcards

I

The roar of cannon rolls from Bulgaria dense and broad,
resounds upon the mountain crest, then hesitates and ceases;
the maned sky runs above; but recoils the neighing road;
and men and beasts are tangled, and wagon, thought and load.
You're deep and constant in me despite this turbulence
and glowing in my conscience, forever still, intense
and silent like an angel when wondering he sees
destruction, or like beetles entombed in dying trees.

II

Nine kilometres from here, look! the haystacks
and homes consumed in blaze,
the peasants smoke in silence by the meadow
and huddle in a daze.
But here, the shepherdess leaves in the water
light ripples in her wake
and gently dipping down, her curly flock drinks
the clouds up in the lake.

III

The oxen slaver red saliva. People
pass urine mixed with blood. My squadron stands
disorganized in filthy bunches. Death
blows overhead its cold, infernal breath.

IV

I tumble near his body. It turns over
already taut like string about to break.
Shot through the nape. *You too will end up like that,*
I mutter to myself. *Lie calm. Be patient.*
The flower of death unfolds in fear. I wait.
Blood mixed with dirt grows clotted on my ear.
I hear a soldier quip: *He'll get away yet.*

Frigyes Karinthy

Struggle For Life

Let's face it, mate, you've been brought down
by every law and trick, that's clear –
The jackals have picked up your scent.
Hungry crows are circling near.

T'was not the pack to prove the stronger,
far meaner beasts have brought you there –
Will feral dogs or humble sparrows
share the feast? I do not care.

You rarely raised your fist and always
halted halfway to the blow –
Was that for goodness, fear or weakness?
Or shyness? Pride? I do not know.

Perhaps disgust. I calm down. Amen.
I do not curse. I don't condemn.
I'd rather be consumed by vermin
than I should ever feed on them.

András Mezei

Grace

How tranquil are
Your children
starving to the bone...

shuffling to Your throne
beyond despair and hurt:

spare for them,
my gracious Lord,
the odd clean shirt!

Eszter Forrai

Petals

in memoriam Janusz Korczak

You were a witness, an author,
a doctor seeking a salve,
a tender, meek protector
true to the end through danger
and even the gas –
and even the gas.

You wove a garland of petals
and flung it high in the sky
above the billowing ashen
smoke that withered
the human smile.

You rose with your petals,
rocking in slumber, draped
in a dreamlike blanket of fables.
You flew with the rows
of your dead, and the babes
became angels.

András Mezei

The Survivor

I: Hanged: A Sketch

He held a fiddle in his left,
a goose brought down, its long limp neck
hung black in death – and to this day
I sense its silenced vocal cords.

What he was not allowed to say
what we can never comprehend
is played out by a hoary bow
upon the slackened silver strings

drawn by the Angel of Good Death
in flight above the snowbound fields:
blue frost upon his grizzled beard
and bunkers and *Arbeit macht frei...*

And still that violin plays on.
Its melody will never cease.
I see a bald, a silver skull.
I bless my father's silver bones.

II: My Father: A Legend

That very death
that very corpse
defines the district
like a plumb-rule
in true suspended
perpendicular.

That measuring-cord
of all of life,
its snowbound plane
and stark protrusions,
projects all human
suffering through
a line across
eternity.

This line so straight –
like weighted down rope
or stretched out cord
or lifting smoke,
a yearning darkened
silver line
through which the body
may rise to reach
its incarnation.

And as a single
beam of light
remains to hold
the tilted head,
the dazzling ray
refines itself
and gains in sharp
intensity.

The beam describes
the path for this
spectacular
one-way procession
of fateful signals:
thus the body
must meekly follow
the faithful breath.

The tightening throat –
the rattling cry –
the fleeing breath –
they liberate
the bursting soul
to rip its road
of focused light
towards the stars,

and cleave apart
our firmament
of deathly darkness,
and find a rest
upon the columns
of air supported
by the Children
of the Light.

The jawbone points
towards the sky –
the shoulder bone
has lost the fiddle –
Above the earth,
beneath the sky
abandoned hangs
a broken corpse
that would not soar
above the hill
of scaffolds, nor would
sink below,
and occupies
the light as though
it were supported
by the soul.

The joints are loosened.
Every bone
acquires its own
and separate weight.
The neck, the limbs
grow elongated.
Like the stars,
the vertebrae
inevitably
pull asunder.

The sagging burden
of the arms
weighs down the shoulders.
The heavy wooden
prison clogs
hung from the feet
extend the ankles,
stretch the knees,
reshape the body.
Death is accomplished.

At last, the final
script of symbols:
The opened mouth,
the hanging tongue
blue like a flower
on a winter twig.
The busy stripes
of the prison garment
come to rest.

Beneath the sky
before the heaven
the flesh, the bones,
the prison rags
disintegrate
and, effortlessly,
the corpse dissolves
within the picture.
And over the desolate
wire fence,
above the fiddler
glows a gentle
protective hand.
Five shafts of light
direct my gaze
towards the City.
And... *Here I am.*

III: Love in Auschwitz

Birdsong, dusk. Departure from Auschwitz.
Resurgent love steps out from the gates,
immortal love whose skeletal essence
could never be consumed by the flames.

Past soaring hopes, reality
slowly settles from the smoke:
the heat of incandescent mess-tins –
a dented spoon beneath the earth –

and like that mouth, that Gothic cavity
that spewed them, gods and fantasies
decompose amidst the dental
gold extracted from the dead.

The gas decays. The bunkers crumble.
The deportation trains withdraw.
And – *Here I am,* and here the arms
to hold the living world in... love.

For love redeems the fence of death:
I share your being and you mine
together in the light and silence
beneath our gagged and distant stars.

Éva Láng

A Shout

*in memoriam Giorgio (Jorge) Perlasca, an Italian Christian who
assumed the mantle of the absent consul from Fascist Spain in
Nazi-occupied Budapest to save more than 5,000 Jewish lives –
including mine*

Well I know the One to thank for
the shafts of light that pierce the darkness.
In the vicious circle of hell
the eye perceives a different world.

The shafts of light that pierce the darkness,
morning born from murderous night.
The eye perceives a different world
when you awake from deadly slumber.

Morning born from murderous night.
Our wounds restored by fresh young sunlight.
When you awake from deadly slumber,
will you enter fresh new worlds?

Our wounds restored by fresh young sunlight
consoling, healing, kissing our hurts?
Will you enter fresh new worlds
if you still trust humanity?

Consoling, healing, kissing? Our hurts
resolved through time? We bear our burden!
If you still trust humanity...
If One questions: who will answer?

Resolved through time? We bear our burden
multiplying in our cells.
If One questions, who will answer
down in this world, and not in heaven?

Multiplying in our cells
the crosses of two millennia.
Down in this world, and not in heaven,
One lives and wipes another's tears.

The crosses of two millennia...
Our bodies marked out and dragged in shame...
One lives and wipes another's tears.
One has eased for me my burden.

Our bodies marked out and dragged in shame,
marked by our star and by our faith...
One has eased for me my burden,
the One who saved the lives of thousands.

Marked by our star and by our faith,
thus our fate has been ennobled.
The One who saved the lives of thousands
is silent...
        I shout in His place.

György Timár

The Bomb Shelter, Afterwards

There was a war and you, small pig-tailed person,
you lost the war by holding on to life.
The roundabout whizzed past: the flaming breath
of its lines of horses spread the stench
of graves. For you, it will persist forever.

Your tightened lips involuntarily twitch.
The skin beneath your eyes turns dark and worn.
You'd dart away – but, like a wounded bird,
you plunge back to the ground you would escape.
Your silence hides a low, unceasing whine.

Our merriment and crisis fineries
invade you like a loathsome, anxious fever.
You can't repel a call for intimacy
though you perceive a film of soiled blood
infecting everything within your touch.

You hide here in the cellars from the world,
whose callous cruelty prevents your healing.
You hesitantly try to re-assemble
the coloured, shiny shards of a piggy-bank:
your shattered childhood. May the pieces fit.

There are no windows here, no skies, no future.
The cellars will be left to store our junk.
I stand above your resting, ruined body.
You fix your gaze on me. Your helplessness
floods over me. I mourn your loss and mine.

Dán Dalmát

Epitaph

Trustworthy traveller, I urge you, tell my fellow Jews
that I've fulfilled the role allotted me by my age.
I was marched with frozen feet along the shores of the Don,
I was pounded by hails of rifle-butt blows in Serbia's mountains.
My broken bones at last have merged with the sane mother earth.
A gust of wind alone reminds my folks of my ghost.
And my good name is lost. And only my guards survive.
And my killers remain in charge… even of my dust.

Judit Tóth

Resurrection

I'm not surrounded by wire fencing
charged with deadly current.
And if I tried to flee, the guard would
not dream of opening fire.

Each night, the chimneys foul the air.
Each night, I burn to ashes.
Each morning reassembles me
broken and astounded.

András Mezei

Keepsakes

I praise my father's compass. He chose to disperse us
to save us the pain of witnessing each other's fate.
That's how I've come to treasure forever these gifts
from my late mother and sister and baby brother:
empty reels, their keepsakes from different camps.

Magda Székely

The Pyre

A terrible throne. It hovers above
the vortex of a pillar of fire.
Instead of seraphs and griffins, small figures
bustle below, their bones aglow.
Their brittle arms: a blighted forest
of flapping wings or flailing rods
gesticulating, lost in space
amidst the silent spokes of light.

The atmosphere grows dense and charged.
A beam shoots out, it tethers the earth
to heaven, tightens, divides into rungs
and becomes a ladder. I hold its base.
Below my feet, the ground gives way.
Above, the heaven, harder than steel.
It rings out sounds in rhythm and rhymes.
Thus sings the chorus of the saved:

Behold, I am holy and holy and holy,
devoid of flesh, comprising gas
and soap and gas and soap and gas
...holy and clothed in loathsome glory.

Each face: a yearning flame in the fire.
But who can recognize such faces?
The very sky is burning, burning...
ablaze with our naked decay of life.
And even she is among these cherubs,
these ruined cherubs of thirty kilos,
and even I cannot pick out her face
among six million flickering faces.

The ladder draws me. Radiant rungs
invite me upwards step by step
towards the flames of the heavenly pyre.
The ladder is leading into the fire
away from its narrowing base, the soil.
...And I'm seized by fear that drags
me upwards. I resist in vain.
I sink my teeth and pain and life
into the altar's glowing embers.

Six million incandescent columns
of ore, like urns, consumed in the flames,
and who can say which was whose mother?
The fire licks and coils and leaps,
engulfing my bones. Behold, I'm here
beyond ravines, past hills, all obstacles,
and here I stand ablaze with them:
ablaze... for they are also burning.

Ágnes Gergely

Beneath Pannonia's Sky

The road turns by the press-house and a white
mud village greets me huddling to the right,

blue winding polished hill road that I see
with an intruder's curiosity

with not a soul just trees and tidy lines
of modest homes with aerials and vines

past wine vaults and beneath Pannonia's sky
a grey prophet – a little donkey – ambles by

she waves back with a mother-of-pearl ear –
the prosperous plebeian class dwelled here

when carts of travelling merchants left a track
along these gentle hills five centuries back:

calm bakers of brown loaves and honey-bread
they watched above the mounting thunderhead

behind them a castle resounded with music and dance
of the Renaissance with Italian elegance

and roads took root wherever their carts would ply
their trundling trade beneath Pannonia's sky –

in his brown caftan tightly wrapped, one day
my own forefather might have walked this way

and where I stand he might have glanced and slowed
his pace to preach with caution by the road

perhaps that other one, more sober, plain
made fancy saffian footwear by the lane

as his wife with amber eyes surveyed the ground
and kept her guard against a hostile hound

and a toddler played about her gathering
herbs from these very slopes and she would sing –

their psalms and their tanned leathers' scent would fill
the air and travel far beyond the hill

surviving winters, with the gales they flew
and from the maggots' entrails rose anew...

these lands caress them softly like a shroud
they came unasked and graceful like a cloud

they were, as I protect and hold to my
own soil, protected by Pannonia's sky:

both ways the road winds blue beyond your span
so leave this land and run, run... if you can.

Magda Székely

Precipice

A human being who managed
a hearty lunch, or observed
in comfort from the kerbside
the neighbours' shrunken faces
during their faltering march,
isolated, deserted,
herded in hatred towards
the killing fields by the Danube –

how could such a person tell
upon what appalling shores,
and over what gaping abyss
I guard against missing a step
and what tenacious powers
tie me still to this place,
and what is the weight I must
carry in isolation?

I'm holding such human beings,
in truth, alone in my arms,
and if no-one prevents my fall
and if my strength should fail
and the final crumb of compassion
should at last be lost...
if no-one comes to my aid,
the abyss will swallow us all.

Éva Láng

Wandering Jews

a new Hebrew Psalm

We do not reopen our wounds
and do not exhibit our wounds
and do not parade our wounds
and do not embellish our wounds
and do not inflame our wounds
and do not inflame our memories
and do not bewail our memories
and do not lament our memories –
for that would not lighten our burden
and would not heal our wounds
and would not lighten our memories
and would not comfort our souls.

Our altars all crumbled to dust
our psalms were chocked on ash
our altars lost their lustre
our altars, the future, died.

Our temples all collapsed
the arks of covenant broke
our psalms soared high towards heaven
our homes were smashed into earth.

And thus our bones were broken
our consciousness tormented
our memories tormented,
our vertebrates were grinded
as our murderers grew wild
and our altars crumbled to dust
and our psalms, they lost their lustre.

And thus our infants fell silent
and thus our men folk grew lame
as the women were lit like torches
and our ancient prayers fell silent
and all, but all met the flames.

The streets took away our sons
the streets, they chased our daughters
the streets, they stoned our sons
the stones, they guarded our dead
while our infants turned into dust
as our murderers have dispersed,
confessed and gained forgiveness
to kill and confess again
and raise righteous gifts for charity
thus robbing the future, the faithful
whose children have turned into dust,
the dust we still breathe in the air:
and as long as we breathe, demand
an account for every deed.

No, we were not more guilty
nor our daughters more attractive
nor our sons any wiser than others –
no, we were only more wretched.
The hearts of our foes swelled with loathing
when they thought they attacked us for love
as they cast aside their faith
as they cast aside their humanity.

Our lips refrain from cursing.
We know the entire truth
and the slander of two millennia
which has infected the world
which has denied the one God,
the God whom we gave to the world.

They hate us for shunning judgment
and trying to live worthy lives,
for having a grip on the world
with some who have still survived,
for showing compassion, not hatred,
for learning to reach into space
for sowing the deserts green and
for navigating the seas.

There is no escaping from us,
no shelter even in heaven,
for we are at home in the universe:
wandering Jews, we'll live forever.

Thomas Ország-Land

Meetings

in memoriam Kurt Waldheim

Small world, what, Excellency? We shall not shake hands.
I do not care how you manage to live with the murder of children
among the conquered women and spoilt vineyards and olivegroves
back in the Balkans, back in your youth: that is your affair.
But what you have done, to me and my world, that's mine.

At last, our final meeting... You were once an obedient officer
ordered to make a corpse of me, perforce a small one.
I have survived the mayhem to make a poem of you.
I am more generous than you and far more consistent.
Old soldiers like you in public life can still be of use.

Admit the past for the sake of the future, and go in peace
at the mercy of your smouldering, sordid, meandering memories.
Or dare to persist in denying the truth and the value of life,
pretend that nothing occurred to stir your attention,
and I promise you will never escape the stench of corpses:

for I will record your name as well as the crimes
from which you say you averted your indifferent eyes,
in tales of horror to be recounted throughout the ages
till the end of the march of innocent future generations
to weigh up anew, again and again, and recoil from your life.

András Mezei

The Wound of Manhattan: A Prayer for Peace

I: The Horror

Oh – the ashes! Dissolved in them, in the ruins
of our Twin Towers of Babel, merge forever
the sacred dust of the slain... and their slayers.

Humanity! Your name is being abused
again to justify mass murder for freedom,
democracy, goodness and God... whichever god.
Appoint for the killers safe cities to hide and to heal
because, devoid of a personal grudge, they turn
themselves into bombs to explode a Holocaust
of random rage, destroying themselves with others
they do not bother to count or comprehend.

The rage of the world has accumulated, distorting
the beauty of life, the planet, the human face.
Unhealing, our wounds gape festering in the cities.
Blood seeps in, and silence, beneath our thresholds.
As the sap withdraws from a winter-chilled tree,
so the lights of our culture retreat below ground.

The worldwide web sags limp in our digital newsrooms.
But the news is stark and manifest: if we
trample down the soft black earth of the molehills,
the soft new Holocaust ashes may fill our mouths.

From the ashes, arises the psalm of our time:
Yesterday, the killers dug up the sacred
bones of our dead and boiled them up for soap.
Today, our own society harvests the blackened
scraps of our corpses for industrial use...
God of the Jews! and Jesus! and Allah! Whoever!
...they can tolerate this, as long as we will.

II: A Prayer

My God, this Holocaust burns up your very domain,
the land where the predator does not detest the prey
but desires it, where the eyes of the carnivore
are green as the grass, and the satiated lion
peaceably roams alongside the trusting lamb –
Gather a handful of ashes from the grounds
of our ruined Towers of Babel, my Lord! and grant that
they wipe away the rage from the bloody, disfigured,
sweat-drenched face of humanity, Your own image
that lives by slaughter and by inheritance.

For there is no hatred left in the ashes... I know that.
For sacred are the remains of people, and pure
the marks of the Lord and the people left in the ashes.

III: America

Mourning Manhattan, daughter of America:
squat down on your stiletto heels in the ashes,
their tender, soft, rich dust, and summon a jeweller
to fashion the ashes into bracelets and rings
to advertise your magnetic wealth and might,
and a necklace with a medallion adorned
by your lovely profile in high relief,
like the raised security print on a banknote.

You ruled the world from your twin towers of trade,
and wore a mantle of glass that swallowed the light
but did not reflect an image. From the multitude
of immigrants' boats, we marvelled at your dark,
magnificent, impenetrable sunglasses.

Your super-fast lifts transported the passengers
up from our sea-levels to the waters of heaven.
And even the traders of the ancient world
still lift their envious gaze towards your shores
across the millennia. Fleets of sunken galleys would
gladly rise from the depths to bring you their cargoes
because you too have become a mainmast, America!

Collect the surviving gems of Solomon's treasure
from the Holocaust ashes! They want to please you.

And so do the wines congealed in the lost amphorae,
the necklets, pendants and crowns of the Queen of Sheba,
and all the world's data that seek to advise you of goods
on offer... and goods in demand. *We must sail on* –
your traders' message will soon be bounced between
the planets across the electric storms of space.

Your frontiers today embrace the celestial bodies.
You have adapted our oars of Biblical craftsmanship
to navigating your solar-powered spacecraft.

Your dainty shoes, Manhattan, have walked the moon.
Your enterprise is admired by all the world.
Even your enemies share your loss of the towers
whose wealthy trading floors collapsed with the dreams
of profits entertained by warrior merchants
who have hung up their shields and helmets and swords
in your spirit: *Wage no war – but trade!*

The towers of their ambition will rise again
and their conflicting dreams and schemes and tongues
will merge in a language of common comprehension.

IV: The Merchant

Manhattan, humanity that you've led to the moon
still trusts you to define our shared ambitions.
If you still are the spiritual tower
of our freedom, support our wretched masses
and give us sanctuary! and give us work! and
give us a chance against our tyrants! Your answer
to our prayers must be pure, as pure as the ashes.

...And learn again, Manhattan, how to run business!
Those who have eyes and ears can see and hear:
good merchants welcome and protect the strangers.

They do not rob them. They dust and wash their feet,
and offer them tea and sweets and fragrant seeds,
because the safety of home and business depends
upon the security of every road.

When they display their goods on offer, their spirit
ennobles their merchandise, for they love the essence
of trade as well as its substance... And thus the merchants
lead their customers past the sand-dunes of commerce
towards the mutual pleasure of a good bargain.

Such endeavours survive any suicide bomb
because the God of the Jews and Jesus and Mohamed
sails with the flying carpet of Aladdin's spirit.

V: The Advice

This is how an ancient teacher and trusted
business consultant put it: *If in your greed
you add house to house and join field to field,
then you will be left to dwell alone in the land.*

And he went on demanding: *How dare you crush
and grind the faces of the poor into dust?*

The faces, the eyes, the mouths, the dreams of the poor
are all your markets, Manhattan, you must protect them!
Leave the poor something worth saving. Return to them
a third of your profits. Dampen the embers of rage.

And learn to respect humanity's loss in the sacred
dust of even the slayers as well as the slain.

Thomas Ország-Land

War Correspondent

for James Fenton

Floating among the ice, these peaceful
soft, curly shapes reflect the sky.
The river rocks them lightly, gently,
their pace appearing slow and graceful
beneath the evening's silver mantle.
We cannot see the fish below, but
discern from here a place of worship
that dominates this wounded landscape.

The fish cannot disturb the dead.
Indifferent, the murdered lie
swelling our rivers of history.
A friendly warlord has purged a delicate
threatening issue of principles
(which we regret). You must have heard:
a war afar stirs passions once
it has occurred on television.

They've left behind a tidy village
of great importance – once, to them,
the toil of ruined generations,
a scent of sweat, the stench of fear,
spent cartridges trampled into the snow
and children recoiled from adult ways,
potential witnesses still in hiding
in crumpled bedrooms (which we regret).

Others I know marched calmly at gunpoint
and left their clothes and shoes on the shore.
They were received by the surging waves
tied in pairs to prevent survival,
to float forever towards the sea
– rejected by oblivion.
We have erected a monument
to urge humanity: *Never Again!*

...A monument secured by our stubborn
pillars of fear that make us insane and
succumb to the lure of the tranquil river.
The icy current coils beyond
our will and wailing. Hear this dirge
composed for you and me, undated.
It mourns the living. We calculate
our fate in sums of overkill.

András Mezei

A Prophet's Final Advice

Thus Theodor said:
My, you have grown!
you're on your own –

But don't you, dudes,
do a dud... deed,
while I am dead.

Magda Székely

The Sentence

I can't relent, for I am alive in the place
of those who can't forgive or change with time:
the slain... awaiting justice as obstinately
as stones are weighing down the earth.

But spring is bright. I eat, and I have grown.
My living flesh would reach towards the living.
I'd like to train my life around mundane
events like plants around a garden post –

yet must remain as resolutely faithful
and strain as unflinching as the dead are dead.
I must remain, like stones upon the earth,
unshaken in our righteousness.

Earth slowly heals the void left by their lives.
Their moaning spaces fill with new arrivals.
Their footprints disappear. My own survival
alone remains the last indictment.

Thomas Ország-Land

The Name

'Hunt down the killers and respect the innocence of their offspring.'
Randolph L. Braham

My name is Eichmann the son, I'm not the monster.
You may relax your face. I am your age
and you and I both share my father's shame.
D'you think you're innocent? I'm responsible
for my father's deeds just as you are for yours.
I am condemned by my inheritance,
the trains and Auschwitz. So is all humanity.
I must embrace my place and role, and bear
my name for I can rearrange the past
no more than you can change your skeleton.

He looked like me, though younger. He was warm,
he loved his children, women, fun and flowers.
He obeyed in full the exterminating state
and thought in terms of tame processing quotas.
Perhaps he managed to avert his eyes
from the purpose of the national enterprise –
perhaps he was, like his entire nation,
hysterically drunk with fear and hatred –
or, like me, he thought he must fulfil his role –
He is condemned for lacking exceptional courage.

And did he love the stench of burning flesh?
He was a man of the stopwatch, not the gun,
an author only of railway timetables, an architect
of ovens only and chimneys, a planner translating
the people's will to kill into detailed instruction,
a man of industry only doing his job.
He thus extended human experience by learning
to channel rage and passion into detachment
and patient dedication to a purpose
beyond a person's modest comprehension.

Today we know we all need exceptional courage
and all of us must answer for our souls.
I am a German, an heir to Goethe's poetry,
a European, heir to the dream of Erasmus,
a Christian, heir to the faith of Jesus the Jew.
I am condemned to keep alive the name
that must confront humanity with our fearful
capacity for suicidal detachment
as well as love. My role is to enhance
our common inclination to choose survival.

Magda Székely

Tablets of Stone

I

The past was horrible. Harsh rules
were imposed and quickly scrapped.
Live declarations writ in stone
and on the cross lit up the minds.
The roar of looming, cloven skies
shook the bones of timorous prophets.
Columns of fire and brilliant visions
illuminated the deserts' gloom.

Far more confounding is the present.
Jonah defied the word of God,
but recognized the voice. He knew
the task, the flesh, the town, the desert.
Tarshish and Niniveh, sibling cities,
like eggs, today they look alike...
Can you tell if you're fleeing one, or
embarking on your task in the other?

These days, the sky turns grey. Divine
revelations fail to move us.
We wage our wars in silence. The voices
of cherished heralds don't assist us.
Unaided, we must comprehend
our tasks in life and death – and if
we do not raise our voice in time
all earth and sky may perish with us.

II

Surrounded by the desert's dust,
I feed on locusts and rare grasses.
The sound of breakers has retreated
along the distant, sandy beaches.
The leviathan spared me. But the heavens
yield no manna for my sake.
Above my head, a burning crown.
Relentless sunshine beats me down.

My words are arid like the landscape.
There's hope for help in every person
moved by the wish to warn the people
to mend their ways and to avert
the certainty of retribution.
But with the most appalling horror
discharged already in the past,
there is no caution left to issue.

There's nothing more compelling than
a nightmare that has come to pass.
Each night, I guard a silent field
of bones beneath a broken altar.
The corpses hold me in their gaze
and I, who have survived alone,
must raise my voice. Words cannot help,
but they must not remain unspoken.

Thomas Ország-Land

A Birth

for Frank Barnaby

How distant: like vultures. The multiplying patrol
of military satellites encircles
the green and throbbing earth in patient precision.
And all has been said. And nothing has been resolved.
Our leaders are lost. The poets stare in silence.

The conference halls are filled with warnings defining
in glaring blindness the final peril of war.
The libraries are the mass graves of our finest words
prescribing cautious strategies for survival.
Our mindless means have soared beyond our purpose.

The priests have lowered their gaze. They watch the countdown.
Our missiles are primed and humming: aimed at ourselves.

Is this the conclusion, the end of all the millennia,
the logical ending never intended? – My love,
come hold my hand, let's call the children together
and lay the table, my love, and crown the hour
because the earth is giving birth to the future.

This is the end of the era of blood-drenched towers.
Humanity (you and I and the neighbours) must choose
how to use our marvellous powers – and either die
by our science or fulfil the ancient ideal
and deploy our plans to tame and enrich this planet.

And the choice is there in the simple logic of children,
the warmth of your hand and even in these very lines.

Thomas Ország-Land

The Jolly Joker of Jerusalem

First things first when
the holy books burst
and lime pits are planned
in this thirsty, troubled
land of passion
and beauty and flavour,
and the mind is mined
for the Cruising craze
and the neighbours pray
and bray and fast
for the festival roast...
as, cool as a fool,
I scribble this treble rhyme
while I'm able.

My first duty
to myself and my host
at this generous table
is to test and taste
and toast and savour
and rejoice in my time,
in the feast of this day
that I might have missed,
even if I was
born to burn
at the end of this line...
like a star, like the joker,
in history's
final, feeble fable.

Thomas Ország-Land

When Hatred Rules

When hatred rules the nations,
I choose without regret
to be a refugee
among the patriots.

Notes

Caution
Jaroslav Ježek was the probable author of lines recalled by survivors of a Nazi death camp at Mauthausen, Austria, and which form the basis of this poem.

Saving the Sodomites
Sodom was a proverbial city of wickedness whose destruction by divine wrath is described in the Book of Genesis.

The Germans' Mercenaries
Georg von Frundsberg (1473-1528) was a German warrior, whose name was adopted by a panzer division of the Waffen SS, the multi-ethnic fighting force of the German Nazi Party. The historical setting of this poem – published anonymously in 1937 in protest against Hungary's alliance with Nazi Germany – was intended to deflect the wrath of the authorities.

The Truth
This poem, composed in 1942 in outrage at the psychological preparation of society to commit mass murder, was probably the author's last. But it was followed by *The Smell of Humans: A Memoir of the Holocaust in Hungary*, one of the greatest narratives to chronicle that tragedy.

The Bull
This poem was the poet's response to Hitler becoming German Chancellor in 1933.

The Witness
Red, white and green are the colours of the Hungarian national flag.

Spark
This was Hanna Szenes' last testimony before her murder.

Steps

Eszter Forrai was a child survivor of the Holocaust who witnessed the massacre of children described in this poem after running away from the march leading to the killing fields on the Danube. The translator was another intended victim of the same mass murder.

Struggle for Life

According to Holocaust legends, this poem was read to a group of starved, naked and brutalized civilian captives – orthodox Jews observing strict dietary rules – to calm and comfort them before their mass execution in a gas chamber.

Petals

Janusz Korczak was a Jewish-Polish physician and author (1878/9-1942). He declined an offer of sanctuary during the Holocaust in order to stay in charge of an orphanage in the Warsaw Ghetto. He was murdered at the Treblinka extermination camp together with the children and staff of the orphanage.

Love in Auschwitz

'Then I heard the voice of the Lord saying, Whom shall I send?... And I said, Here am I. Send me!' Isaiah 6:8.

Meetings

Kurt Waldheim (1918-2007) was an intelligence officer of Hitler's Wehrmacht, later President of Austria and secretary-general of the United Nations; he died peacefully days after publicly repenting his silence over the atrocities.

The Advice

'How dare you crush and grind the faces of the poor into dust?' Isaiah, 3:15.

A Prophet's Final Advice

Theodor Herzl (1806-1904) was the Jewish-Hungarian founder of modern Israel.

Tablets of Stone

In the Book of Jonah, a prophet dispatched to Niniveh sought to shirk his task by escaping to Tarshish.

The Poets

Many of the authors whose works are translated or quoted in this book are the recipients of the highest state honours bestowed by Hungary. But literary prizes are frequently granted by the Hungarian state on the basis of political rather than literary considerations. The following biographies do not include such prizes. This is in line with the decision of several outstanding writers who have recently declined or returned their decorations in protest over the populist educational and cultural policies of the present, ultra-Conservative Hungarian government.

Dán Dalmát (b.1934). Poet, translator and librarian. He emigrated to Israel in 1968 after winning a literary reputation on the staff of a Budapest satirical journal. Today he writes in Hebrew and translates Hebrew literature into Hungarian.

György Faludy (1910-2006). A towering figure of European literature described throughout his prolific writing career as the reigning king of Hungarian poetry. He spent much of his life in political imprisonment or exile. As the Nazis advanced across Europe in WW2, Faludy retreated via Paris and North Africa to the United States where he served the Free Hungary Movement as its honorary secretary and enlisted with the American Air Force to fight in the Far East. He returned to Hungary after the war to be imprisoned and tortured by the Communists. In his second exile after the the doomed 1956 anti-Soviet revolution, he edited a literary journal in London, taught at Columbia University in New York and received a Pulitzer Prize as well as an honorary doctorate from the University of Toronto. He was nominated for a literary Nobel and later awarded the Salvatore Quasimodo memorial prize. He went home again to post-Communist Hungary to emerge as an eduring source of controversay adored by a doggedly loyal public and still loathed by the illiberal political and literary establishment. The city of Toronto recently adopted him as its own poet and named after him a small park beneath the apartment where he had spent 14 years of his exile.

Tamás Emőd (1888-1938). Poet, playwright and theatre director, a master of the light touch and gripping drama, loved by the public but all but forgotten by literary editors.

Eszter Forrai (b. 1938). Poet and painter, lives in Paris. Her many literary prizes include the *Prix Academie des Lettres et des Arts de Perigord*, the *Prix Edmond Genest* and *Prix Athanor*.

Ágnes Gergely (b. 1933). Poet, translator, novelist, scholar. A proud descendant of generations of rabbis and men of letters, she was one of the first major Hungarian writers to explore in public print during the Soviet era the long-suppressed experience of East European Holocaust survivors. Her many literary awards include the Salvatore Quasimodo memorial prize.

Jenő Heltai (1871-1957). Poet, translator, dramatist and novelist, a master of light verse and poignant humour that earned him membership in the *Légion d'Honneur.* His huge output remains fresh and in demand as ever. He declined an invitation extended to him by his uncle Theodor Hezl – the founder of the modern state of Israel – to join the Zioniost movement by declaring his exclusive loyalty to Hungary. He later also declined a rare offer of immunity from anti-Semitic legislation, made during the war by the racist Hungarian authorities in recognition of his service to literature. His works were ignored for many years under the subsequent Communist cultural administration but enjoyed sustained popularity.

Frigyes Karinthy (1887-1938). Poet, translator and novelist, a recipient of the Baumgarten prize. He was a satirist of enormous international influence – even though the fireworks of his verbal wit have translated poorly into other languages.

Éva Láng (b. 1925). Poet and journalist who has released a fury of Holocaust verse only during recent years.

András Mezei (1930-2008). Poet, publisher, journalist and major chronicler of the Holocaust. He survived the Nazi rule of Hungary in the Budapest ghetto where some 17,000 souls perished around him from hunger, disease and the fancy of uniformed bandits. He trained as a locksmith after the war and emigrated to Israel as a youth, but returned to his homeland to emerge as a prominent voice of the Soviet era and an influential participant of the post-Communist reconstruction. He served as president of the Hungarian-Israeli Friendship Society for many years and won the Israeli Kotzetnik prize. His Holocaust poetry is widely read and taught in English translation but heavily ignored by Hungary's literary and cultural establishment.

Thomas Ország-Land (b. 1938). He is a poet and foreign correspondent who writes for global syndication from London and his native Budapest. He survived the Holocaust as a Jewish child hiding from both the Nazis and the Allied bombers. He participated in the 1956 anti-Soviet revolution; later he read philosophy at Acadia University in Canada under Watson Kirkconnel, the great-grandfather of Hungarian literary translation into English, and trained on *United Press International* in Montreal and *The Times* and *The Financial Times* of London.

Miklós Radnóti (1909-1944). Perhaps the greatest among the Holocaust poets. He fell victim to a mass murder of Jews at the close of WW2, staged by a unit of the regular Hungarian Army, while displaying a white armband signifying his well documented, sincere conversion to Catholicism. Some months later, the exhumation of the grave turned up a small notebook found on his body containing poetry written in even handwriting and complete with printers' instructions, recording the chaos and brutality of the Holocaust in magnificent classical metre. The poems are winning a robust international reputation in English translation. They have also made Radnóti a beloved national figure in Hungary – although his books were recently torched by neo-Nazi demonstrators. He was a recipient of the Baumgarten prize.

Magda Székely (1936-2007). Poet, translator, literary editor. She was the lifelong teacher, muse and collaborator as well as the wife of András Mezei (above). A shy and very private person with relatively little published output, she is still hardly known beyond Hungary. Yet she is one of the greatest Holocaust poets. Her literary awards include the Salvatore Quasimodo memorial prize.

Hanna Szenes (1921-1944). Poet, farm labourer, soldier. She emigrated as a youth to Palestine to escape rising Fascism in Europe and eventually joined the British Army there. She was parachuted into partisan-held territory in Croatia from where she trekked to neighbouring Hungary with a dual mission to rescue downed Allied aircrews and assist the Zionist resistance to the annihilation of Jews. She was betrayed, imprisoned, tortured and murdered. She is revered as a war hero; her songs, mostly about love, faith and nature, are sung the world over.

Ernő Szép (1884-1953). Poet and novelist and for long a fashionable journalist and playwright. *The Smell of Humans: A Memoir of the Holocaust in Hungary,* his eyewitness testimony of forced labour and gratuitous cruelty at the hands of the Nazi rabble, is a treasure of Hungarian literature hardly known in Hungary. But it has been ably translated into English by John Bátki (see Further Reading). Szép survived the horror to die in deep poverty – some say he starved to death – alone and forgotten, after the war during the Soviet era.

Vera Szöllős (b. 1937). Poet and short-story writer published mostly in Hebrew and her native Hungarian. Her recurring themes are survival through the Holocaust as well as the grim years of Soviet administration that followed.

György Timár (1929-2003). Poet, translator and journalist and the recipient of many literary prizes including the *Claude Sernet award*.

Judit Tóth (b. 1936). Poet, translator, editor, novelist, academic who lives in Paris and visits her native Budapest very seldom. Her poetry is dominated by the horrors of the Holocaust, which orphaned her, as well as the loneliness of exile. She holds the Robert Graves prize for poetry.

István Vas (1910-1991). Poet, translator, editor, a descendent of generations of provincial rabbis. He was a Catholic convert, like his close friend Radnóti (see above). He survived the Holocaust in hiding with friends in Budapest. This enabled him to record in poetic eye-witness accounts the events of the Nazi rule, including the deportation of his own mother to a place of mass murder. His many literary prizes included the Baumgarten award.

Further Reading

Thanks are due to the editors of the following publications and academics at the following institutions for editing, publishing, teaching or exhibiting early versions of some of these poems: *Acumen, Ambit, The Jerusalem Report, Maecenas Press, New English Review, Pennine Platform, the Penniless Press, Snakeskin, Stand* and *The Tern Press* as well as the Universities of Dallas, East Anglia, Edinburgh, Elte/Budapest and San Francisco.

For more work by these and other Holocaust authors available in English, and for more information about the experience of the Hungarian Jewish and Roma peoples during the Second World War, see the following:

Neil Astley (ed.) *The Hundred Years' War: Modern War Poems*, Bloodaxe Books, UK, 2014

John Bierman, *Righteous Gentile*, Penguin Books, London, 1981

George Eisen, *Children and Play in the Holocaust: Games among the Shadows*, Massachusetts University Press, 1988 and Corvina Press, Budapest 1990

Kinga Frojimovics *et. al, Jewish Budapest: Monuments, Rites, History*, Central European University Press, Budapest, 1999

Ágnes Gergely, *Requiem for a Sunbird: Forty Poems* (trans. Bruce Berlind *et al.*) Maecenas Press, Budapest, 1997

György Faludy, *My Happy Days in Hell* (trans. Kathleen Szász), Penguin Modern Classics, London, 2010

György Faludy, *37 Vers/37 Poems* (trans. Peter Zollman), Maecenas, 2010

György Faludy, *Selected Poems* (trans. and ed. Robin Skelton), University of Georgia Press, Athens, 1985

György Faludy, *Learn This Poem of Mine by Heart* (ed. John Robert Colombo), Dundurn Books, Toronto, 1983

György Faludy, *East and West* (ed. John Robert Colombo) Hounslow Press Toronto, 1978

Mari and George Gomori, (eds.) *I Lived on This Earth*, (trans. George Szirtes *et al.*) Alba, London, 2012

Imre Kertesz, *Fateless*, Vintage, London, 2006

Randolph L. Braham (edited with an introduction by Elie Wiesel) *The Geographical Encyclopaedia of the Holocaust in Hungary,*

Northwestern University Press, the US Holocaust Memorial Museum and the Rosenthal Institute for Holocaust Studies at the Graduate Centre, City University of New York, 2013

Randolph L. Braham, *Bibliography of the Holocaust in Hungary,* Columbia University Press and the Rosenthal Institute, 2012

Martin Gilbert, *Churchill and the Jews,* Simon and Schuster, London, 2007

Martin Gilbert, *The Holocaust,* Holt, Rinehart and Winston, New York, 1985

Desmond Graham (ed.) *Poetry of the Second World War: An International Anthology* Chatto and Windus, London, 1995

Thomas Kabdebo (ed.) *Hundred Hungarian Poems,* Albion Editions, Manchester, 1976

Frigyes Karinthy, *A Journey Round My Skull* (trans. Vernon Duckworth Baker) Corvina, 1992

George Konrád, *A Guest in my Own Country: A Hungarian Life* (trans. Jim Tucker, ed. Michael Henry Heim), The Other Press Books, New York, 2007

George Konrád, *A Feast in the Garden* (Trans. Imre Goldstein), Harcourt, New York, 1992

Paul Lendvai, *Hungary between Democracy and Authoritarianism* (trans. Keith Chester) Hurst, London, 2012

Paul Lendvai, *The Hungarians: A Thousand Years of Victory in Defeat* (trans. Ann Major) Hurst, 2003

Adam Makkai (ed.) *In Quest of the Miracle Stag: an Anthology of Hungarian Poetry from the 13th Century to the Present,* Atlantis-Centaur, Chicago, 2003

Kati Márton, *Enemies of the People: My Family's Journey to America,* Simon and Schuster, New York, 2009

Kati Márton *The Great Escape: Nine Jews who Fled Hitler and Changed the World* Simon and Schuster, 2006

Kati Márton *Wallenberg: Missing Hero,* Random House, 1982

András Mezei, *Christmas in Auschwitz* (trans. and ed. Thomas Ország-Land) Smokestack Books, UK, 2010

András Mezei, *Holocaust 1944-2004* (trans. Dániel Dányi, Thomas Ország-Land and Jon Tarnoc), Belvárosi Press, Budapest, 2004

András Mezei, *The Miracle Worker* (trans. Thomas Kabdebo), Belvárosi, 1999

Julie Orringer, *The Invisible Bridge,* Penguin, 2011

Thomas Ország-Land, *Berlin Proposal*, Envoi Poets Press, Newport, Wales, 1992

Thomas Ország-Land, *Free Women*, National Poetry Foundation, Fareham, England, 1991

Thomas Ország-Land, *The Seasons*, Tern Press, Market Drayton, England, 1980

Zsuzsanna Ozsváth, *When the Danube Ran Red*, Syracuse University Press, New York, 2010

Zsuzsanna Ozsváth, *In the Footsteps of Orpheus: The Life and Times of Miklós Radnóti*, Indiana University Press, Bloomington, 2000

Zsuzsanna Ozsváth and Frederick Turner (trans. and ed.) *Light within the Shade: Eight Hundred Years of Hungarian Poetry*, Syracuse, 2014

Alfred Pasternak, *Inhuman Research: Medical Experiments in German Concentration Camps*, Akadémiai Press, Budapest, 2006

Patricia and William Oxley (eds.) *Modern Poets of Europe*, Spiny Babbler, Kathmandu, 2003

Katalin Pécsi (ed.), *Salty Coffee: Untold Stories by Jewish Women* (trans. Ágnes Merényi *et al.*) Novella Press, Budapest, 2004

Monica Porter, *Deadly Carousel*, Quartet Books, London, 1990

Miklós Radnóti, *Deathmarch* (trans. Thomas Ország-Land), The Penniless Press and Snakeskin, both in England, 2009

Miklós Radnóti, *Foaming Sky* (trans. Zsuzsanna Ozsváth and Frederick Turner), Princeton University Press, 1992 and Corvnia, 2002

Hilda Schiff (ed.), *Holocaust Poetry*, Fount Paperbacks, London, 1995

Ernő Szép, *The Smell of Humans: A Memoir of the Holocaust in Hungary* (trans. John Bátki), Central European University Press, 1994

István Tótfalusi (ed. and trans.) *The Maecenas Anthology of Living Hungarian Poetry*, Maecenas, 1997

Krisztián Ungváry, *Battle for Budapest: 100 Days in World War II* (trans. Ladislus Löb), I. B. Tauris, London, 2003

Miklós Vajda (ed.) *Modern Hungarian Poetry*, Columbia University Press, New York, 1977